Path to Productivity

A Guide to Reclaim Your Time
and
Do More of What You Want

Talina Sen Smet

Path to Productivity

A Guide to Reclaim Your Time and Do More of What You Want

Copyright © 2018 by Talina Sen Smet

Printed in Canada

First Printing, 2018

www.Productivity-Master.com

*To my dogs, Sydney and El,
who have given me pure joy
since the moment we met.*

This book is a must read for those of us who attend annual sessions in goal setting, business planning and time management but do nothing differently year after year to ultimately achieve the same results. Path to Productivity has just synthesized for me a very large volume of material into clearly laid out actionable steps in a very no-nonsense practice. I felt encouraged and motivated while reading this book and can see how doing the same thing year over year will not drive a new result but making some specific committed adjustments will.

- Judy B., Financial Planner

Path to Productivity is an extremely helpful book and a must read for anyone who strives to better themselves in terms of productivity. It is written simply and concisely and lays out a clear plan of action with some really helpful tools and suggestions. The author provides amazing insight into efficiency and success and is perfect for kids in middle school to adults.

- Aarti Sabharwal, Student

Path to Productivity is highly recommended for anyone that is interested in improving productivity and overall quality of life. It is a beneficial wake up call to anyone that is finding themselves stuck in a routine of poor day-to-day habits. The book's straight forward approach makes it easy to internalize the information provided and make positive and lasting changes.

- Calvin V., Program Manager

Path to Productivity teaches us that by following simple steps you can significantly change your life for the better. Path to Productivity explains what can be blocking us from working productively and how we can be efficient in finishing our work. This book is recommended to all people seeking to improve their mental state and work quality.

- Jason Gupta, Student

Contents

As a gift, I would like to offer you the audio version of my book for free.

Simply go to **www.productivity-master.com** to claim your audiobook! Here, you can find more productvity resources for free!

Introduction

One million people search the internet for information about productivity every single month. But you are one of the few who decided to actually do something about it. Congratulations! Establishing effective productivity habits is a well-known path to success in all areas of life.

Obviously, there are many online resources for increasing your productivity, whether in the form of blogs, YouTube videos, or even books. So why should you read this one?

This book is short, simple, and easy to understand. It is filled with practical steps that can be implemented almost immediately, so you will be able to see improvements in your productivity right away!

The strategies in the book are well thought out and proven to be effective. I am aware that everyone has a busy life, and I truly value your time, so I have condensed these strategies into six chapters that each conclude with an action summary to get you started quickly. By reading this book, you save yourself the time and hassle of combing through thousands of articles and wasting many unnecessary hours.

I wrote this book as a result of my experiences and the experiences of others. My friends constantly tell me that they are not being productive, yet nobody seems to take action. We go through our day-to-day lives being bored by what we are doing and not getting anything done. We sit at our desks doing meaningless work or listening to nonstop lectures. And we go home so tired from the day that we don't have the energy to change our lives. We all want to be productive in general, but on a day-to-day basis, we are swamped with so many tasks, deadlines, and responsibilities that we never get around to it. This book is your step-by-step guide to finally improving and optimizing your productivity.

> *We go through our day-to-day lives being bored by what we are doing and not getting anything done. We sit at our desks doing meaningless work or listening to nonstop lectures. And we go home so tired from the day that we don't have the energy to change our lives.*

How amazing would it be if you could transform your life into one where you have the energy to not only get your work done, but to have fun as well? What if you could create habits that leave you consistently energized and rarely stressed? What if you could easily identify your passions and use them to create a career you love?

Stop for a moment and imagine a life where you are doing the things you love without the stress of money or deadlines, because everything has already been completed. Imagine having the time to travel or spend time with your friends and family, or even just learn a new skill like playing an instrument or mastering a foreign language. Wouldn't life be so much more exciting?

By following the easy-to-complete steps I've laid out for you in this book, you can complete as much in the first hour of your day as you now do in the entire workday. My book gives you six strategic pillars for becoming more productive and less stressed, so you can live a more balanced and happy life.

This book is actionable, not theoretical. It provides you with the tools you need to start increasing your productivity now. It won't leave you more confused than you were before, as some books do. It provides clear and defined answers to the many questions about productivity.

But before we get into the details, you will need some brief background information on the brain, so you can understand how specific environmental factors affect us.

First, your brain releases chemicals called neurotransmitters. These are responsible for your emotions—for instance, dopamine for motivation, serotonin for happiness, cortisol for stress, and oxytocin for love. I will be mentioning these neurotransmitters throughout the book.

Second, each of our brains consists of billions of neural pathways. These pathways are like roads in your brain. When you think a new thought or practice a new skill repeatedly, you are paving a new road. For example, if you learned to ride a bike when you were a kid, it's likely you still know how. That's because you practiced so many times that you created a superhighway / pathway in your brain.

We need to learn new productivity skills to create new neural pathways. Our goal is to intentionally build productivity highways by practicing every day. That way we'll establish a plethora of neural highways where information flows at a super-productive rate—so that being productive is almost automatic for us.

The more you practice, the more efficient the highway. But usually developing these new pathways can feel a bit strange when you first start. This is normal. Be kind to yourself and encourage yourself to practice, even though it may feel uncomfortable. A note of caution: typically, it is this discomfort that makes us stop practicing, so please stay with it, and the discomfort will fade. When you feel discomfort, take a breath and remind yourself why you're making the changes—for a more balanced, efficient, and fulfilling life.

Remember, being productive doesn't mean working all the time. You can be dedicated to your work, but your goal is to work efficiently so you can have more time to spend with your friends or family, or doing anything else you want.

As you head into the first chapter of this book, I want to wish you well, and I really hope you'll use the strategies in this book to change your life for the better!

1 | Environment

Ⅰn the first chapter, you'll learn how your environment can help or hurt your productivity—and how to create your own perfect working environment so you can excel!

It's amazing how much our physical environment affects our work quality and efficiency, even though we rarely consciously notice our environment. That's because our brains try to filter out all the extraneous stimuli so we can focus on one task. If our brains didn't do this, we would be unable to focus, because we would be constantly distracted by the sound of our own breathing, the air-conditioning, or the cars going by.

Right now as you read this, your brain is filtering out the patter of the rain or the traffic outside so you can focus on this book. But as we know, some brains are better at doing this than others. (You know who you are!) So we need to tailor our environments to allow our brains to function optimally. Once we have eliminated distractions and added the items that improve our productivity, we'll be ready to start developing productive habits.

So let's begin by making sure all aspects of our environment are working with us, not against us. This section looks at how our bodies, minds, and senses are affected by our environment.

Touch

AIR TEMPERATURE

Believe it or not, the temperature of your environment affects the quality and efficiency of your work. Cooler temperatures are perfect for keeping us alert and awake, whereas warmer temperatures soothe us and make us happy. To give yourself the best working environment possible, it's helpful to have a balance between warm and cool. I recommend a temperature of approximately 18 degrees Celsius or 65 degrees Fahrenheit. This is a comfortable temperature that will still keep you alert, focused, and ready to work.

However, it's really important to know yourself. Everything I tell you in this book will vary from person to person. The best way to find a temperature that works for you is to try a range of different temperatures and see which one is most effective.

POSTURE

Having good posture actually has several benefits for you and your productivity. Sitting up straight allows your lungs to fill to their full capacity, so more oxygen flows through your body faster. Oxygen keeps our brains working, keeps us alert, and keeps us focused on the task at hand. Getting a full breath of air can be like drinking water after a long run. We often don't notice that we aren't taking full breaths until we are so oxygen deprived that we are almost falling asleep. Then when we take a deep breath of air, we instantly wake up and feel more energized.

Your body indicates to your brain how to feel and respond. For example, sitting up straight with a smile sends signals to your brain that you are happy (obviously!), and slouching with a frown tells your brain that you are upset. In response, your brain releases the appropriate neurotransmitters (named in the Introduction) to create that feeling of happiness, sadness, or another emotion.Have you ever heard anyone say that if you just smile, you will automatically feel happier? This is because every time you force yourself to truly smile, even if you're not feeling happy, your brain releases serotonin and dopamine, the chemicals responsible for the feeling of happiness.

Now that you know the science behind how your body affects your mood, you are ready to start implementing it. And guess what? It's super easy! Every time you come to your workstation, follow these steps to put yourself into the correct mindset to work:

1. Smile—and your brain will reward you with dopamine, the happy motivational neurotransmitter! And the great news is, if you do this often enough, your brain will remember to reward you every time you sit down to work! You will feel an automatic rush of dopamine as soon as you smile.

2. Sit up straight. Adjust your chair so it supports you in maintaining good posture. Sitting up straight increases

the oxygen in your lungs and blood flow to your brain, so you'll feel more energized, alert, and ready to complete your work.

3. And while the most common way of working in today's society is to sit at a desk, it's not the only or even the best way. There are other options that modern offices are introducing that can be implemented easily at home—for example, the standing desk.

One day when I was feeling super unproductive and lazy, I tried something new that I had only read about in articles . . . I stood up! Wow, what a strange phenomenon. I took my laptop and placed it on top of a $5 Ikea box I had lying around—and what I experienced was amazing! I was more productive in that one hour than I had been for the past two days. While working standing up, I not only felt more energized and alert, but also got rid of my back pain from sitting all day! I highly recommend using standing desks (or even just a box on top of a desk), especially if you want to make a substantial change within the same work area.

Sight

Sight is the sense we use most in our day-to-day lives. The surroundings we see affect our mood and alertness, which in turn affects the quality of our work. In this section, you'll learn how to change your visual environment so it provides you with motivation and inspiration instead of depressing you.

LIGHTING

One essential piece of your environment is lighting—specifically natural lighting. It is proven that when you work in conditions where there is ample natural light, you will be significantly more productive and energized. In fact, under poor or artificial lighting conditions, your cortisol levels rise. Cortisol is the chemical responsible for stress. And if you are more stressed, you are less productive. (You will learn more about how to reduce stress in chapter 5).

In general, we're most productive when there is abundant natural light and less artificial light. For example, I like to get things done in the morning because nothing feels better than working under the flood of natural morning light through the window—and then being *done* working for the day! However, your most productive time of day may be different depending on your personality—you could be a night owl or an early bird. It is important to do what feels right for you.

> **"**I like to get things done in the morning because nothing feels better than working under the flood of natural morning light through the window—and then being done working for the day!

Whatever your schedule, how can you capture more natural light? One way is to work near large windows so you get the most light possible. If you do the majority of your work in the morning, you will want an east-facing window; likewise, if most of your work is done in the afternoon or evening, a west-facing window is best. Position your desk so that the window is perpendicular to your computer screen. A window directly in front of or behind your screen can cause eyestrain. In addition, lighter wallpaper/paint colours are more effective in reflecting natural light, resulting in a brighter room.

However, if you aren't able to modify your working environment to this extent, don't get discouraged—this step will not make or break your productivity level. As long as you have some access to natural light, you will be creating a better working environment. Here's a tip: work outside whenever you can. You will get optimal natural light along with fresh air! If you can't work outside, consider a 10-minute break to get some fresh air.

In contrast to natural lighting, light *pollution* (bright light at night) can have negative effects on our sleep cycles, which in turn can affect overall productivity. The circadian rhythm is our internal alarm clock. It releases selective hormones and neurotransmitters depending on the time of day (i.e., cortisol in the morning and melatonin in the evening). Our brains absorb cues from the colour spectrum in daylight. Basically, your circadian rhythm tells you when to sleep and when to wake up, depending on the light it detects. This is why you generally get tired when it is dark (at night) and why you wake up during the daytime. An excess of light pollution can disrupt this cycle, thus creating an irregular sleep cycle. Lack of sleep can be extremely detrimental to your learning capabilities and mental well-being, including your overall happiness and satisfaction with life.

INSPIRATION

In addition to natural lighting, it is extremely important to create a space that you want to work in. So inspire yourself—and motivate yourself. What drives you? Why are you doing this work? You need to create a space that embodies these feelings. I recommend putting up pictures of your inspiration or motivation on the wall. The pictures could be related to a goal (see chapter 3) or reminders of family, friends, pets, vacations, or anything else that makes you happy. Modify your environment to whatever degree you are able. Paint the walls to make yourself happier if that's an option, or keep a guitar in the corner to play during a break (if that is an option for you). Or even simply put some inspiring pictures on your desk. Make your work space a place you want to be! You want it to put a smile on your face as soon as you walk in.

Personally, I have several pictures of past vacations and of me with friends on my wall. I also have my guitars and a map to give me a break from the stress and remind me why I'm doing this work: so I can eventually be successful and travel and see new places!

> *So inspire yourself—and motivate yourself. What drives you? Why are you doing this work?*

I recognize that some of you who work in an office are unable to modify your working environment. But do your best to try to make your environment enjoyable, even if you are unable to modify it on a large scale.

Creating an environment that you enjoy and would want to work in is really the most important takeaway.

Sound

DISTRACTING NOISES

Noise has a significant effect on productivity levels. A study by the University of Nebraska showed that people's performance scores on a test decreased when they were exposed to annoying or irritating noises. But you probably already knew this. Have you ever been in a loud classroom and just wanted to scream at everyone to be quiet because you were trying to concentrate and get your work done? Well, I have, and it is extremely frustrating.

Some people like to work alone, as they are less distracted and do their best work when they are by themselves. Others find motivation and inspiration in being surrounded by their peers as they work. They are most productive when they're close to the energy of others. Just make sure you won't get distracted. (Don't lie to yourself!)

I would recommend a quiet place where you will be uninterrupted as the best work environment. But if you like to work amid the energy of others, then an office or library may be best. A coffee shop is OK as long as you are not subjected to interruptions and you have noise-cancelling headphones. What you need to do is find the space that works for you.

For those who work better in general when alone, a bedroom is a quiet option, although it's helpful to have an area that is dedicated specifically to working (a desk). It's not ideal to work on your bed; you need defined areas for rest and work so that you aren't tempted to switch between work and rest easily. Another option is a home or work office.

And while it is important to remember that noise contributes to lower productivity, it's also important not to isolate yourself from your peers. Learning how to work in groups and in a classroom or open office environment is an extremely helpful skill. Working alongside peers is beneficial in many ways. For example, an MRI study showed that in stressful situations, stress is lowered when you are connected to another human being. So being able to focus while in the presence of others is extremely useful.

Later in the book you will learn more about how to create habits that improve your focus. You will learn to focus in any environment, so you can be flexible with working conditions that are not ideal but are temporary. A good example is having to complete a project in an airport, where you aren't able to modify your environment in any significant way.

MUSIC

One controversial topic is music. I prefer to listen to music while I work because it puts me in a good mood. If you are not in a good mood when working, it is likely you'll be more frustrated, and therefore, less productive. Music stimulates peptides in the brain that produce endorphins, specifically dopamine, which aids memory and reduces stress! These endorphins can shift your emotional state and put you in a happier mood.

"Well, perfect then," you say. "I'll just listen to music, and it will automatically increase my productivity!" Well, yes and no. You have to know yourself. You can test whether music helps you or not. While it can be highly beneficial for morale, music can also be highly distracting for some people.

It also depends on what type of task you are trying to complete. Repetitive tasks are made easier and more enjoyable by listening to music. Because music is a pattern of sounds, it will likely increase your productivity when you're doing things like bookkeeping or checking your email (which by the way does not count as being productive. Please stop checking your email multiple times a day—you are severely decreasing your productivity!)

Classical music without words is said to help with work, but music with lyrics is proven to be distracting. Music can, however, block out other bothering factors in your physical environment such as people and background noise.

Alternative forms of incorporating music into your life, such as playing an instrument, can help you socially and intellectually and reduce stress. Singing releases oxytocin, the same neurotransmitter responsible for the feeling of love. About a year and a half ago, I picked up the guitar and taught myself to play using YouTube. For me, it was a great way to relax and have fun. I love the sound of the guitar, and I really wanted to play. This motivated me to put in the effort to learn.

Smell

One interesting thing about smell is that it has a direct link to memory. This is because our memories are dispatched by emotion. Smells send signals directly to the amygdala (which is the emotion center of the brain), and smells bypass the thalamus (the thinking part of the brain where information gets processed). Essentially, smell is taking a shortcut to your memory.

If you have to memorize information quickly, using something scented (like an essential-oil diffuser or candle) will help you memorize faster, which in turn, greatly aids your productivity.

I realized how effective this was when I was using watercolours to sketch while watching Netflix. The next time I encountered the distinct smell of watercolour, that Netflix episode appeared in my head in an instant. Crazy, isn't it?

Clutter - Sensory Overload

Clutter affects all your senses and your ability to process and focus. Just get rid of the clutter and organize your workspace! This one is pretty obvious, yet a lot of people neglect to do it. You will increase your productivity so much if you know where everything you need is and aren't distracted by excess stuff.

Clutter increases stress as your space becomes overwhelming. Some say clutter or a messy desk can be helpful for creativity, but for productivity, it just slows us down. Remember how I said that some brains are better at filtering out external stimuli than others? It applies here too! Having a clean and organized workspace will allow your brain to focus easily and reduce possible distractions. This will allow you to get more done in one sitting, and eliminate the environmental factors that aid procrastination.

Getting rid of clutter also means removing other distractions—including your phone or excessive notebooks and materials. Turn off notifications so you won't be tempted to check your phone while working. Every time you check your phone or are otherwise distracted while you work, you have to do two things that really slow you down: 1) Convince yourself to start working again (which is often the hardest part of the work), and 2) Get back into the mindset of working. You will need to reset your brain and refocus to get back into the same groove you were in before.

> *Every time you check your phone or are otherwise distracted while you work, you have to do two things that really slow you down: 1) Convince yourself to start working again (which is often the hardest part of the work), and 2) Get back into the mindset of working.*

This takes time and effort. By eliminating distractions, you will be more efficient, and you will save yourself the extra work of getting back into the right headspace. If you know that you will still be tempted to check your phone or start doing something else when you are supposed to be working, ask a friend to take your phone from you for a certain time period. Alternatively, there are apps that lock certain social media so you aren't able to access them during a time period that you set. Another option is to put your phone on airplane mode—or set a timer so you can measure how much work you are actually getting done. This removes the choice to procrastinate for you. These measures are often necessary in order to prevent distractions as people begin to switch their habits. Eventually, you will have enough willpower to leave your phone alone without putting it in a different location or mode.

Take Action Summary

After you read this book, you will be ready to start taking action right away by setting short- and long-term goals for your environment. I would advise you to do this right away. Don't wait. Life is busy, and it is inevitable that you will move on and forget that you wanted to do this. Setting your daily routine and goals *right now* is the best way to ensure that you will actually practice these habits:

- Change your air temperature to 18 degrees Celsius (65 degrees Fahrenheit).
- Choose your preferred posture (sitting or standing) and then sit or stand up straight. (Set reminders to do this).
- Work in a place that energizes you.
- Use natural lighting as much as possible.
- Inspire yourself with your surroundings.
- Decrease distracting noises.
- Include music in your life. Even if you don't listen to music as you work, you can use it to relax before or after working.

2 | Mindset

Mindset is a really important tool for productivity. You will be one hundred times more productive if you go into your day with a positive attitude, believing you will be productive. This is one of the most significant chapters because without the right mindset, everything will feel harder than it needs to be.

> 66 *You will be one hundred times more productive if you go into your day with a positive attitude, believing you will be productive.*

Brain States

Before we get into the details of mindset, it's important for you to understand the mental states that are most productive. It has been shown that the "alpha state" is most helpful for visualizing and working. (I'll explain more later in the book.) The alpha state is the balance between meditation and being fully alert, and it's the most effective level of brain frequency. This state creates a space for the clearest thinking, as well as relieving stress, so you can fully engage in your task without becoming stressed. Being in the alpha state will help you focus, which is a key factor for a productive mind.

To get into the alpha state, I recommend meditating in the morning before you start your day. Personally, I do a quick ten- to fifteen-minute yoga session in the morning that concludes with a three-minute meditation. That way, I start my day with exercise, meditation, and a clear and focused mind. But you can skip straight to the breathing exercises described in the Daily Routine section if you are short on time.

The best brain state for learning is the "theta state." It is also known as the "sponge" mode because it enables us to absorb everything around us. Children are often in the theta state. That's why they are able to learn new skills so fast. So if you are learning something new, it's a good idea to get into the theta state. You can do that by getting consistently good sleep and focusing your mind on one subject. In addition, when you are in the alpha state for longer periods, you will naturally transition into the theta state.

Exercising will help you get into a good brain state. Exercise is necessary for your brain to function and develop properly. Along with being energized to do your work, you will reduce your chances of getting diseases like dementia and Alzheimer's in the future and maximize blood flow to your brain. Our ancestors actually developed their brains by running for up to twelve miles a day, so exercise is essential for productivity, brain development, and continued evolution.

A bonus is that the more you exercise, the more pathways will form for your blood to carry oxygen around your body and to your brain. Oxygen in your brain is what energizes your neurons to keep firing, so that you experience the dopamine and serotonin releases needed to get into an optimal brain state and feel motivated. (See more about motivation in chapter 4). In addition, when we exercise, new brain cells form in the hippocampus area of our brains (which helps with memory).

The good news is you can exercise whichever way you want! You can go for a quick jog, do a muscle-toning workout, a HIIT (High-Intensity Interval Training) cardio routine, a dance class, or anything else! Any exercise will help blood flow to your brain and help you concentrate better.

Visualizing

Visualization is an amazing tool that profoundly enhances your ability to be and stay productive. If you were to ask any extremely successful person, you will find that 99 percent of them use visualizations to aid their success on a daily basis. Once you use the ideas above to get into the alpha state, you can begin your visualization. (If you feel you don't have the time for visualization, don't worry—the length of your visualizations is up to you. They could be less than five minutes or longer than an hour! You will learn how to work visualization into your daily schedule in chapter 3.)

Research shows that visualizing upcoming events greatly improves them. For instance, Olympic athletes commonly use visualization before they compete. They picture how their event will go, imagining all the details and perfecting their movements in their minds. This works because it helps your brain understand how you want the performance to go. It's just like practicing a perfect version of the event.

One interesting thing your brain does is it fires the same neurons when you visualize competing as when you are actually competing. So if you visualize enough, the perfect run-through of your event will become like muscle memory to the neurons in your brain, and you will automatically perform better. This is why so many athletes, speakers, singers, and businesspeople practice visualization every day. But visualizing is not only useful for careers that involve a lot of performing—it is applicable to any job. Even daily tasks can be visualized, and will thus go more smoothly!

Once you have found the perfect spot to visualize (e.g., sitting on a yoga mat, at your desk, or sitting on your bed), and you're in the alpha state, start picturing your day. Walk through your entire day in your head. Imagine having an amazing conversation with your friend or colleague; see yourself nailing the job interview; see the expression on your face when your presentation gets a standing ovation. Attempt to visualize all of these things.

To improve your visualizations, try three things to incorporate mind, body, and soul. The first is to create a visualization that's so vivid, colourful, and lifelike that your mind believes you are actually there. As I noted before, the same neurons fire in the brain when we imagine something as when it actually happens to us. This means our brain believes the event is actually happening in both cases. That's how strong visualization can be.

The second step is to incorporate the body by using all your senses in the visualization. Try to imagine cutting the tension in the room with a good joke. Hear everyone laugh. Smell the muffins from the bakery next door. Try to taste the delicious lunch you're going to eat during a meeting where your pitch moves up to the next level of review. Doing all these things will make the visualizations more real. (Don't get discouraged if you are having trouble visualizing with all your senses at first. It takes practice—you will get there).

Finally, to incorporate the soul, feel as if you are there. Try to feel your emotions when you get that promotion. You are smiling uncontrollably, and your heart starts beating out of your chest. You feel a glow and passion inside that you only get every so often, because you know you worked so hard for the promotion. This is how you should feel at the end of every visualization. The feeling you get after your visualizations will motivate you to do them again and again!

After your visualization is complete, you are ready to start your day with a positive attitude and open mind. You will be willing to work harder because you know how it feels to finally receive what you are working so hard for.

Focus

Our brains are very susceptible to distractions, but we have the ability to train our brains to focus. To practice, you need short sessions of complete focus, with no distractions. This means working in a quiet environment, as well as minimizing distractions such as cell phones. There are several apps that you can download to mute distractions and notifications for a designated amount of time. Start with periods of half an hour with no distractions in order to train your brain to focus. Eventually you will be able to work longer without any distractions.

Focus and concentration are based in a network in the brain. Optimum focus occurs when our brains release neurotransmitters such as serotonin. (Serotonin is one of the neurotransmitters that evoke happiness.) That's why when you become emotionally attached and committed to your project, you will find yourself concentrating better.

Being emotionally attached to something will also help you pay attention and memorize better. Do you ever notice that people who *love* their jobs are often very successful, and students do better in subjects they're interested in? So to be truly focused, it is important that you invest yourself in the topic and take an interest in it. Even if you are not particularly interested in the subject (for example, a project in school), you can still invest yourself by feeling grateful that this is the one and only time you will ever have to do that project. Once you find your passion and focus on it, projects won't feel boring again.

Neuroplasticity

Our brains are highly plastic, which means we are able to grow and change constantly, no matter our age. The term for our changing brains is "neuroplasticity."

However, the more we age, the harder it is to change an already-developed neural pathway. This is why it is much easier to learn a new language as a child—and why one of the hardest things to do is to *un*learn something. Our interpretation of each day's events is based on our prior experiences. Everything you have done and encountered in the past has shaped who you are today.

But sometimes we need to rewire our brains in order to open our minds up to new ideas. Every time we think a new thought, our brains physically make a new pathway of neurons, connected by dendrites and axons. Whenever you learn something new or practice a skill, a neural pathway is either formed or strengthened, because the neurons in that path are firing. So practice and repetition are the keys to forming a new habit.

Picture a sled going across fresh snow. The first time it goes over the snow it makes a light groove. And the more times the sled goes over that path, the more distinct and fast the path will get. But if the sled never goes over that path again, the path will just fill back up with snow. By practicing every day, we are able to create and maintain a pathway that's easy and efficient to travel on. If we stop practicing, we start losing the neural pathway, and it will eventually become nonexistent, thus allowing our brains to make room for the pathways we use more frequently.

So now we have a choice to make: keep practicing the bad habits that make us less productive—or form new ones that increase our productivity and well-being. Let's not make our main and strongest pathways the ones that cause us to check our social media every five minutes. Instead, create and strengthen neural pathways that lead to productive habits laid out in the Take Action Summaries in this book.

66*One of the hardest things to do is to unlearn something.*

Remember to keep an open mind when learning these new techniques. If you believe you aren't cut out to be productive, you'll never be productive—unless you change your mindset. If you send a message out into the universe, that message wants to manifest itself in reality. So if you say you will be productive to-day—even if you don't fully believe it—you will be, because your subconscious wants to play out what it hears.

If you are unfamiliar with the role your subconscious plays in productivity, listen to this statistic: research shows that 90 percent of our decisions are primarily based on subconscious thoughts acquired when we were young. That's crazy. Nine out of ten actions are already set for you in your subconscious!

That's why it's so effective to put a message out into the world so your subconscious can hear and become familiar with it! To do this, you can repeat self-affirming statements aloud every day, so your subconscious can listen and receive the message.

Concentration

Practice, practice, practice! In order to strengthen neural path-ways, it is essential for us to practice focusing so we can become an expert on focusing and concentrating. Remember when you were a kid and you learned how to ride a bike? It was difficult at first (and you put all your concentration into it) but then it got easier as you practiced more and more. While you practiced, your neural pathways formed and strengthened. And eventually, it didn't take as much focus to get on that bike and keep your balance. So, eventually, that skill turned into muscle memory and it got pushed down into a deeper part of your brain, responsi-ble for more automatic skills. Hence the saying "It's like riding a bike." So now, let's learn to ride a new bike . . . the bike of focus, concentration, and productivity!

Success

Some people have a subconscious fear of success. It may seem a little silly that people fear success, but it's true. We have to let go of the misconception that greater success means more work. And we need to identify what preconceived ideas fed to us as children are holding us back from success now, and get rid of them. We need an open mindset to allow ourselves to grow.

It's important to create a mindset that allows you to strive to be fulfilled. You should always shoot for the stars but be happy with reaching the moon. Be sure to take joy in every little success. If you are constantly striving for more, you will never have time to enjoy what you have. You can't earn happiness—you have to create it. It is a feeling. Always strive for your goals and take action to achieve them. But don't forget to live in the moment.

To figure out what beliefs are holding you back, go through the following questions, and for each one, catch and record the first thought that comes to mind. Often, we can identify negative subconscious thoughts by our first instinctual response. Be honest with yourself and really change your mindset.

1. Do you really want to succeed? Why do you want to succeed?
2. What have you been working for thus far in your life?
3. What is holding you back?

Take Action Summary

- Get into the alpha state.
- Visualize your success.
- Train your brain to focus.
- Let yourself succeed.

Now that you understand how the brain works—and why you should take certain actions to help yourself succeed—the next chapters will show you *how* to take those actions and turn them into results that you'll see in your daily life.

3 | Routine and Planning

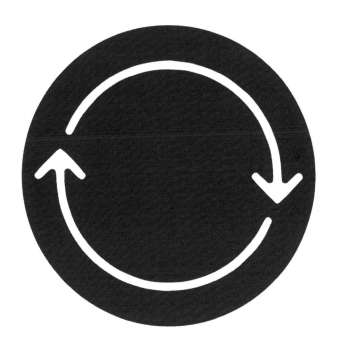

Daily Routine

Scientists say it takes anywhere from twenty-one to sixty-six days to make a habit permanent or automatic. It's best to practice specific elements of productivity every day to become a more productive person overall. In this chapter you will learn about the simple tasks you can complete on a daily basis for greater productivity. A study showed that our brains are 40 percent habit—we are habitual creatures by instinct. This means we don't think before acting on these habits. This can be a good thing or a bad thing. We can continue to watch Netflix or YouTube for hours on end and turn our brains off all day—*or* we can create good habits that will benefit us in the present and future.

KNOW YOURSELF

Throughout this chapter you should not only be reading, but also reflecting on your own experiences to see how you can implement these tools in your life. You may need to adjust what I am telling you to do, because everyone is different. So experiment and do what works for you. If you know that taking a break from exercise for the weekend means you won't go back to it next week, then keep exercising every day of the week. If you know you are not able to sit still for the duration of time I am recommending, start with a shorter time—eventually you'll be able to work up to the recommended time for working without distractions. You need to know yourself and be honest with yourself.

People typically go through a cycle when starting a new skill. They start the new skill and get really excited about it. Then something comes up, and there is a period of time when they can't practice the skill. After that, people do one of two things. They get really hard on themselves because they didn't follow through on their goal, so they stop practicing it altogether. Or they eventually just get bored with the idea or skill and gradually stop doing it. Sound familiar? Well, you're not alone. This is why we need to set schedules that work for us and create fail-proof systems to keep us on track with our goals. Here are some of the best ideas I have seen and tried:

1. Create reminders to practice the skill every day.

   Creating reminders keeps you from being able to use the excuse "Oh, I forgot" or "I didn't have time," because the skill will literally be scheduled into your day as one of your daily goals (see next section).

2. Create a reward system or a way of tracking your skill every day.

   Personally, every month I draw a little daily skill-tracker on a piece of graph paper. I keep it on my desk so I can check off the skill every time I complete it. I love checking things off a to-do list, so this motivates me. It is also a great way to track your skill over the course of a month or even a year. Alternatively, you can find something else to reward yourself with that fits your personality.

3. Make it exciting.

   If you look forward to it, you will make time to do it. If you want to go out with your friends, you have no trouble finding the time. If you want to watch a movie or scroll through Instagram, suddenly you have two hours of free time. Wanting to practice a skill works the same way.

Here are some ways to make learning a new skill exciting:

1. Make a game out of it—test how much you can truly learn in an hour, a sitting, a day, or a week. Try to beat your own score every time!

2. Push through the discomfort—create a habit by learning a little more of the skill every day until it becomes fun naturally! Don't give up!

3. Create a plan to confront yourself and motivate yourself when you inevitably get bored with practicing the skill. Remind yourself why you are doing it. (You can see more on this in chapter 4, Motivation.)

MAKE USE OF YOUR MORNING

You should complete the following tasks every morning. Getting them done before work or school will make your day flow with ease. Completing these tasks will also give you more energy to start your day. Feel free to change the order of the tasks. Do what works for you. (A lot of these tasks are based on *The Miracle Morning* by Hal Elrod. It is an incredible book, and his morning schedule is truly amazing. I highly recommend reading it if you haven't already.)

The first thing you will complete every morning is deep breathing. You can find guided deep breathing and meditation on Spotify or YouTube, or you can follow what I have outlined below:

1. **Take a deep breath in through your nose for four seconds.**
2. **Hold for four seconds while maintaining a good posture.**
3. **Exhale for four seconds through your nose or mouth.**
4. **Pause for four seconds.**
5. **Repeat two more times.**

As you may remember, deep breathing puts you in the alpha state, which is ideal for productive working and studying. Once you get in the alpha state by doing the breathing exercises, it's the perfect time to do the visualization practices that you learned in the last chapter. Remember, the more vivid the visualization, the more effective. Some things you can visualize include your upcoming day, a special event, and short- and long-term goals. (You will learn about setting proper goals in the next section).

While you are still in the alpha state, you can also complete a gratitude practice. Practicing gratitude is not hard. Think about anything you have that you're thankful for and *feel* how grateful you are that it's in your life. This can be anything from a friend or family member to an object or experience. It's really important that you don't just say, "I'm grateful for my dog," or "I'm grateful for my education." You have to truly feel the happiness you have inside when you're with your dog or learning new things. You should really experience it. Visualize it—and feel it. Practicing gratitude releases dopamine, serotonin, and oxytocin—neurochemicals responsible for excitement, happiness, and love.

Personally, I write three things I am grateful for every day in my journal. That way, I can keep track of my gratitude practice each day. It also makes your gratitude more real when you write it down.

Another thing that's really important to do daily is exercise. Even just a five-minute workout, yoga session, or brisk walk is extremely beneficial to your health and productivity. When you exercise, your body releases endorphins, which are chemicals that make you feel happy and reduce the feeling of pain. So if you're not feeling up to doing anything, or you're feeling depressed, exercise is a way to feel more energized and lift your mood. I understand that exercising every day is not easy, but by setting daily goals for yourself, you will be able to build up a habit of exercising so you'll actually want to exercise! Don't try to change your whole lifestyle in one day—because that's obviously not going to happen. You will never be able to sustain a drastic lifestyle change because you will get so exhausted. Instead, create a plan with step-by-step goals for yourself.

Finally, if you want to learn or improve a skill, try quickly practicing it in the morning. Reading, writing, drawing, journaling, or even practicing a musical instrument can be done before you go to work or school. Twenty minutes of practicing a skill every morning is an incredible way to speed up your learning process. It can move mountains for you in the long run.

For some people, morning can be an optimal time to get things done, as energy levels are higher and there are fewer distractions. However, doing these things is helpful any time of day, so try to figure out the time that works best for you.

"When you exercise, your body releases endorphins, which are chemicals that make you feel happy and reduce the feeling of pain."

Don't be overwhelmed if you think this is a lot to do in the morning. You're right—it is, especially if you have a busy life, as we all do. One tip is to set your alarm ten minutes earlier every day for a week, so by the end of the week, you will have over an hour of extra time!

To allow the appropriate amount of time in the morning to do everything you want without being rushed, estimate the time it takes you to complete all these tasks and set your alarm by counting backward from when you have to leave.

Once you know what time you need to get up, it's helpful to use REM sleep cycles to track what time you should go to bed. You don't want your alarm to sound when you are in REM (rapid eye movement) sleep, because it will disturb the most essential portion of your sleep. If you are awakened during this part of your sleep, you won't feel like getting up, and you'll feel more tired than if you were in a different sleep stage.

REM cycles generally follow one-and-a-half-hour increments. By counting backward in one-and-a-half-hour increments from the time your alarm will sound, you can figure out what time to go to bed. If you need to wake up at 7:00 a.m., for example, try going to sleep at 10:00 p.m. or 11:30 p.m. That way you won't wake up in the middle of your sleep cycle.

If you have set aside the time for completing these tasks and find your morning is still overwhelming, you can split some of the tasks between two days and do part of them each day. The two practices I would recommend doing every day, however, are setting goals (see next section) and visualizing. These are really important and fundamental techniques that will greatly boost your overall happiness and productivity, enabling you to get more done while still getting a proper amount of sleep.

I have a friend who just started at a new school. Her previous school started at 8:45 a.m., but at the new school she has to be in class by 7:30 a.m. So she adjusted her schedule—because she had to.

But I'm not asking you to wake up earlier because you have to. I want you to wake up earlier to complete all these things because you *want* to—because you feel it will make a significant difference in your productivity and your life.

I know I am much more accountable to myself if I get things done earlier when I have more energy. But if you don't have enough time in the morning, or you are *really* just not a morning person, don't worry. Just make time to practice good and productive habits at other times of the day, and your productivity will increase.

PLAN YOUR DAY

Planning your day is essential to productivity because it clarifies the steps you will take to achieve your goals for the day. Think about it this way: if you were building your dream home, you wouldn't just pick up a hammer and start hammering away at a piece of wood. That would get you nowhere. Instead, you would lay out the steps you need to take, create a blueprint, and get help from contractors, architects, and possibly interior designers to help your dream home come to life. You need to plan your day with the same care, so each day is a dream day.

PRIORITIZE DAILY TASKS

I like to start the day with a couple of small tasks. This gets the ball rolling early, but keeps me from feeling overwhelmed by big projects at the start of my day. Getting a few checkmarks on your to-do list can put you in a good mood and boost your confidence right as your day is beginning! If you have a lot on your plate, start with a couple of small tasks, then tackle the big ones, and end with any leftover small tasks. I have laid out some sample schedules for different people at different stages in their lives on my website, www.productivity-master.com/resources. Simply click the link to download a free PDF schedule that you can personalize with your own tasks!

Once you are feeling good about the small things, remember to prioritize your work. I like to lay out my work in order of priority on my bed or my desk. I assess priority based on the due date and the importance of each project. For example, if I have a project due in two weeks that will make or break my career, I will complete it before another assignment

"Start the day with a couple of small tasks. This gets the ball rolling early, but keeps me from feeling overwhelmed by big projects at the start of my day.

that is due in a week. One other way to judge priority is to see which tasks are stressing you out the most. If you have a task that you know would feel amazing to get off your shoulders, complete it first!

There's actually a great rule for prioritizing: the 80/20 rule. It means that 20 percent of your time and effort will produce 80 percent of your results. So each day, figure out the 20 percent of tasks that will contribute the most to achieving your goals, and make those your top priority. Through this process, you can rule out checking your email more than twice a day and scrolling through social media when you have work scheduled. Basically, stop doing busywork and start working on things that matter. If you want to learn about this technique in depth, I would recommend checking out Richard Koch's books. I have included links in the further reading section of the book.

STICK TO THE ROUTINE - USUALLY

I've given you some tips for your mornings and daily routine, but make sure your routine is something you want to do. Adapt it to your personality. Make it fun and stick to it. But remember, you are allowed to change up your schedule once in a while. Especially if you are the type who gets bored with routine, it's important to switch the order of things or start practicing a new skill—just try something new! Sometimes breaking the routine can be a change for the better! Just don't forget to practice every day—or very regularly—so you can form good habits.

Setting Goals

There are two main aspects of goals: duration (short-term or long-term) and quality (simple or extraordinary).

In this section, you will learn how to set both short-term and long-term goals that are amazing and realistic. In the chart below, I show the types of goals that would fall into each category. At the end of this chapter I have provided you with a blank template of this chart. You can also download a free blank template by visiting my website www.productivity-master.com/resources.

Please take the time to fill out the chart with your own goals. This will provide the clarity you need to set definitive goals. The chart below follows an acronym called LESS, allowing you to better categorize your goals and to learn how to plan and execute the different types of goals. The acronym LESS signifies that by following these categories, you can achieve your goals in LESS time!

Goal Setting: LESS System	SIMPLE	EXTRAORDINARY
SHORT-TERM	• Daily tasks • School/work assignments • Daily practices (yoga, exercise, eating healthy food) • Practicing a musical instrument or other creative skill	• Do small things that will contribute to long-term goals. • Find the joy in little things that you do on a daily or weekly basis (dance class, taking a walk with your grandparents, volunteering at a senior home, being more present in life). • Socialize/go out to connect with friends.
LONG-TERM	• Create good habits. • Do daily tasks long-term. • Practice a skill every day so it becomes a lifestyle habit. • Eat healthy food long-term. • Exercise every day or multiple times per week.	• Determine career dreams. • Choose places you want to travel. • Set life goals. • Set retirement goals. • Plan for buying a home. • Set family goals (dating, getting married, having kids, etc.).

LESS:
Long-term
Extraordinary
Simple
Short-term

45

SHORT-TERM AND SIMPLE

Short-Term and Simple goals are those you can accomplish in a relatively short amount of time, such as a day or a week. You should set daily goals for each day. I recommend committing a specific amount of time to setting your goals for the day every morning. Alternatively, you can schedule time in the evening to set goals for the next day. Create your checklist on a piece of paper or on a whiteboard. This will help you stay motivated and schedule your time wisely. Determine how long it will take to accomplish each goal, and set a realistic number of things you will accomplish that day. Personally, I have a whiteboard on my wall where I write down what needs to get done by the end of the day on one side, and the week's schedule on the other side. Below is a replica of the whiteboard.

Monday (1st)	Tuesday (2nd)	Wednesday (3rd)	To Do (Priority Order)
			Task #1- Due Monday
			Task #2 - Due Tuesday
			Task #3 - Due Wednesday
			Task #4 - Due Thursday
			Task #5 - Due Friday
			Task #6 - Due Monday (8th)
			Other minor tasks
			...
Thursday (4th)	Friday (5th)	Saturday (6th)	
		Sunday (7th)	
			Today's Date: Monday, September 1st

Remember, daily goals are fairly easy to set. They're just everything that you need and want to get done that day. But one common mistake is to just *think* about the things you want to get done, instead of writing them down. To keep yourself organized and on track, it is absolutely essential to write out your goals and have defined deadlines. This will not only benefit you right now, but will also help build the habit of effective time management that's necessary for any career. Deadlines make life easier because we have been trained to get things done by a deadline. So please set deadlines, and have a friend hold you accountable. In chapter 4, Motivation, I will elaborate more on the "Productivity Buddy" accountability system I have created.

SHORT-TERM AND EXTRAORDINARY

Short-Term and Extraordinary goals are small things that will help you in the long run. They could be anything from attending a brainstorming meeting to get ideas for improving your business, to just going out to meet new people and make connections. These goals may not seem very necessary, but they are really important when you look at the long-term benefits.

To set these types of goals, you need to have your end goal in mind (your long-term and extraordinary goals). If you know your end goal and the specific time frame for completing your long-term goal, you can break it down into the steps necessary to reach the goal. Those steps are your Short-Term and Extraordinary goals! For example, if your end goal is to run a successful business, your Short-Term and Extraordinary Goals would include the brainstorming sessions you set time aside for.

LONG-TERM AND SIMPLE

Long-Term and Simple goals are small goals that will be repeated and will eventually become habits. As you learned earlier, you can train your brain to create good, productive habits. Long-Term and Simple goals are, quite frankly, the most boring. These are repetitive tasks that you complete day after day. But this is how habits are formed. Without these goals, it will be extremely difficult to change the way you live on a day-to-day basis and to become a more productive and fulfilled version of yourself.

LONG-TERM AND EXTRAORDINARY

Setting Long-Term and Extraordinary goals is very different from setting simple goals. Simple goals are highly realistic and tend to be boring and tedious. Long-Term and Extraordinary goals are adventurous, fun, extreme, and amazing. Personally, I love setting these goals. It motivates me and lets me think about my future.

Long-term goals can be set monthly, annually, and for a longer period of time (like five or ten years). If you haven't made a bucket list yet, I advise that you do. It's a fun way to spend some free time—and it will actually benefit you in the future. It lets you experience the feeling of setting goals that are ridiculously amazing. On my bucket list, for example, I have a list of places I want to see, things I want to do, and experiences I want to have, as well as my career goals. Setting these long-term goals is extremely important because you will be inspired to achieve them.

Monthly long-term goals can be things like exercising for a certain number of hours (since being healthy energizes you and can even cause you to be happy overall) or completing a big project. Annual goals can be earning enough money to go on vacation. And longer-term goals can be graduating, buying a house, or even growing your business to reach a specified number of sales by a certain deadline.

You need to make sure all your goals are SMART, but in the case of Extraordinary goals, you want to make them SMART-I: Specific, Measurable, Achievable, Relevant, Time Limited, and Inspiring. Specify exactly what the goal is and how it is going to benefit you.

Let's say your goal is to start a successful small business. First, you need to make it measurable. Does success mean acquiring a certain number of customers? Reaching a certain dollar amount in revenue or profits?

Next, you need to make sure the goal is achievable. Is it reasonable? Don't expect to make a million dollars in your first month. Make your goals realistic, and create a plan to achieve them. Eventually, with time, you will get to your million-dollar mark.

Now, is your goal relevant? Is it going to help your life overall? Make small goals that are relevant so you can eventually achieve a big goal. You can do this by laying out a timeline with micro-goals

48

that are easily obtainable.

This brings you to time limited. Set a deadline for each micro-goal. This is a really important part. You can say, "In one month, I want to have a specific number of clients/sales/profits/ etc."

Finally, make your goal inspiring. Personally, I believe that this is the most important part. If you don't feel excited about starting a business, it's likely you won't be motivated to do the hard work that's necessary to get going. Making your goals inspiring will motivate you to start. Use this inspiration as momentum to take action toward your goal now!

If you are able to use your goals to inspire yourself to work hard, your productivity will increase significantly. One way to turn your goals into motivation is to print out images of what you are working toward—(e.g., a car, house, pet, instrument, vacation, etc.)—and use them to create a dream board that reminds you why you're doing all this. A dream board consists of pictures and quotes that inspire you and remind you of your goal. It can be put up in your bedroom, office, or other work space. You can also use it as the background for your phone or laptop. Seeing it will help motivate you to work hard.

IT'S OK TO SAY NO

One thing I have learned in the past few years is that it's OK to say no. You only have so much time. Although this book will help you make better use of it, time is still limited. So learn to say no to certain things. Just because there is an opportunity, it doesn't mean you are obligated to take it. You need to learn to be selective about your commitments and to not feel guilty about declining an offer to join another club or go to another networking event. Use your long-term goals to identify what you want to focus on, and then make that your main priority. Setting these long-term goals is extremely important because you will be inspired to achieve them.

Goal Setting: LESS System	SIMPLE	EXTRAORDINARY
SHORT-TERM		
LONG-TERM		

Take Action Summary

- Create a daily routine and incorporate these priorities:
  - Deep breathing/meditation to get in the alpha state
  - Visualization of your day and goals
  - Gratitude
  - Exercise
  - Practicing new skills
  - Sleep
- Plan your day in writing.
- Learn to prioritize tasks.
- Learn to set goals using the LESS system (use the chart below).
- Say no when necessary, so you can stay focused on your priorities.
- Ensure you have SMART-I Goals

4 | Motivation

Train Your Brain

Self-motivation, in my opinion, is one of the most valuable skills to have, because if you have the will to accomplish something, you will be able to do it. So it's helpful to understand how self-motivation actually works.

The science behind motivation starts with a neurotransmitter called dopamine. When your brain senses that something important is going to happen, it releases dopamine throughout the brain and nervous system. With this boost of dopamine, we feel a burst of reward and positive energy within us. Training your brain with dopamine is like conditioning a dog to do a trick for a treat, because even if the dog doesn't get the treat, a release of dopamine still occurs in anticipation. When the dog sits, you give him/her a treat as a reward, and eventually, when you command your dog to sit, he/she will sit without needing a treat as an incentive. This is because neurotransmitters responsible for happiness and satisfaction are released BEFORE the actual event occurs. Basically, when the dog's brain thinks, "Wow, I'm about to get a treat, how great is this?!" the brain sends a signal to release the neurotransmitter dopamine. So the dog will feel happy even before being given the treat.

Using this same method, humans can motivate themselves to start working—which is often one of the most difficult parts of doing a task—and can also train themselves to keep at it and stay on task.

> *People who are naturally more self-motivated actually have more dopamine releases than others, or are more sensitive to dopamine.*

People who are naturally more self-motivated actually have more dopamine releases than others, or are more sensitive to dopamine. Interestingly, introverts are more sensitive to dopamine releases than extroverts are. So it takes less dopamine to motivate/excite introverts than to do the same for extroverts.

Now, you may be saying, well, that all sounds great, but how do I actually train my brain to do that? There are a couple of simple things that can greatly increase your self-motivation and allow you to "feel like working":

1. Work in the same environment every day, and make it an environment that excites you or makes you feel happy. That way, your brain will release dopamine every time you sit down to work, and before you even get anything done, you will feel happy. (However, if you can't find an ideal place, your environment won't make or break your productivity. See the next tip.)

2. Fully experience your pride and joy after completing a really hard task. You will be motivated to work harder if you are able to remember the good feeling of being done with a job. Ask yourself this: What do I think about when I say the word "work"? Do you think about having to sit at your desk for hours on end, completing tedious tasks that bore you? Or do you picture the feeling you get after you have done the work? Most likely you are picturing the first one. What you need to do is change your mindset to remember the amazing feeling of completing all your work. This way you will be motivated to start your work right away.

Don't worry if you have trouble starting to work at first—this is completely normal, and you will learn why in the next section. The good news, remember, is that your brain is highly plastic. Neuroplasticity means your brain is constantly changing and forming new pathways as you learn and grow. This is why you can successfully learn a new skill! So trust neuroplasticity, and remember that neurons form stronger pathways as you practice the skill, making it feel easier and easier to do.

Remember, too, it's unrealistic to think you will automatically be motivated all the time by just following these steps. To be truly motivated, you need to do something meaningful for you and others. See chapter 6 on Passion to find out more about this.

Long-Term vs. Short-Term Thinking

Our ancestors only had one thing in mind—staying alive. So they sought opportunities that would give them an immediate reward (a release of dopamine). This could be anything from spotting an animal to kill for food to winning an attractive mate. Both these things trigger an immediate release of dopamine. The problem is that in modern society, many things that provide immediate dopamine releases are not very good for us—for instance, gambling, eating sugar, or thrill-seeking. Although we're modern-day beings, our brains haven't learned to recognize that we need to work hard toward a long-term goal in order to significantly improve our lives.

Our brains will tempt us with things that provide an immediate release of dopamine, but it's essential that we resist the urge to eat that piece of cake or watch "just one more" YouTube video. By resisting the urge to seek immediate dopamine releases, we are training our brains to focus on long-term goals that will actually benefit our lives as a whole. Instead, keep the bigger picture in mind—how this action will affect your life. Will it have a positive or negative impact on your life as a whole?

This is not to say, however, that you aren't allowed to have any fun. By all means, go out for an ice cream once in a while; go to an amusement park and get your dopamine release. But doing these things on a regular basis trains your brain to seek immediate dopamine releases, and leads to a decrease in your health and productivity.

> *By resisting the urge to seek immediate dopamine releases, we are training our brains to focus on long-term goals that will actually benefit our lives as a whole.*

However, there is one way to make your craving for that dopamine-rush benefit you: give yourself things to look forward to *after* you have completed your work. Just as it motivated the dog to work for a treat, this will stimulate an immediate dopamine release and motivate you to do your work.

Support

When learning a new skill, it is always a good idea to build a support system. So start first by finding a "productivity buddy." This is someone who will learn the new skills with you—or someone who can support you throughout your journey to increased productivity and make sure you don't quit when it gets hard.

Your productivity buddy can be someone you've known for a long time or someone you just met. You can both follow all the steps in this book or complete my course on productivity together. It's similar to bringing a friend to the gym so you can motivate each other to exercise, rather than sitting at home on your phone.

Your productivity buddy can also be someone you can share your progress with—someone who will help you recognize how far you've come on your journey and keep you motivated the whole time! If you can't think of anyone you can do this with, that's OK. That's why I've created a Facebook group for all the readers of Path to Productivity. Join the group through the link www.facebook.com/ProductivityMasters.

All you have to do is post to the group, saying that you are new and you're looking for a productivity buddy. Someone will volunteer, or I will match you with someone.

Second, it is important to make your goals public. It may be scary to let everyone know you're working to change and improve your habits so you can create a more productive life, because you worry you might let everyone down or be embarrassed. But the good thing is, this fear will actually motivate you to stay on track with your journey to productivity.

Procrastination

Fun fact: procrastination is a survival skill our ancestors developed to keep from doing difficult tasks that were risky or dangerous: procrastination kept them safer. In modern times, however, procrastination mostly causes us to be unproductive and has a negative, rather than positive, impact on our lives. So we need to evolve with the times.

> *Fun fact: procrastination is a survival skill our ancestors developed to keep from doing difficult tasks that were risky or dangerous: procrastination kept them safer.*

Here are several different ways to overcome procrastination:

1. Stop. One way to stop procrastinating is to just start working. Go cold turkey on procrastination or go on a procrastination diet. Start your tasks right when you get to work/school or home from work/school. Create rewards for sticking to the schedule or punish yourself for not sticking to the schedule—the carrot or stick approach. (And eventually, your success and free time will be a reward in itself.)

2. Challenge yourself. Set challenges for yourself. For example, you can say, "I bet I can't start my tasks at home right after I get home from work, and finish them before dinner, every day this week."

3. Catch yourself. If and when you feel yourself slipping back into habits of procrastination, remind yourself why you are making this change. Do a quick visualization and imagine your end goal. See yourself achieving it, and feel all the good feelings you would have. This will motivate you to start your work and get it done.

4. Get excited. Use excitement as momentum for getting started. Have you ever noticed that when you are excited about a new project, you start on it right away? You need to create that excitement as momentum to get you started on every task you commit to.

Believe

It's funny how simple things can be if we let them. If we believe we can do something, we can do it. If we believe we're not cut out to accomplish that task, it won't be accomplished. It is as simple as that. All you have to do is truly believe that you will accomplish your goals. Once you believe it, say it or write it down, and you will automatically start working toward that goal.

This is not to say that it is effortless. It isn't. But believing in your goal sends a message to your subconscious to start working toward it. I want to leave this chapter with a quote by Saint Augustine that summarizes this chapter perfectly: "Pray as though everything depended on God. Work as though everything depended on you." It doesn't have to be about God. It can be whatever you believe in—the universe, the subconscious, science, etc. Believe it will all work out. But work as if everything were up to you.

Take Action Summary

- Train your brain to self-motivate.
- Work toward long-term success, not short-term satisfaction.
- Create a support system—find a productivity buddy.
- Push through procrastination.
- Practice concentration and focus.
- Believe in yourself.

5 | De-Stress

Talina Sen Smet

Relaxation

One important yet simple way of de-stressing is to find ways to just relax and turn off your brain ... Schedule time for this! Relaxing and making sure you are replenished is just as important as actually working. That's not to say I'm commending you for bingeing Netflix for fourteen hours straight. But in moderation, relaxation is really important. So you need to find ways that you can relax and replenish, and then schedule that into your day.

I learned this the hard way. I am the type of person who likes to just get my tasks done and then have time to relax later. I am an extremist. I would work really hard one day, and then the next day do literally nothing, because I felt "I deserved a break." This is not a good way of doing things, as I learned throughout my high school experience. You'll be a lot more productive if you work for a reasonable amount of time each day and give yourself consistent breaks, rather than working the entire day or week straight, and then doing almost nothing for the next three days or a week.

This is especially true if you are a student preparing for exams. Start studying early—or at least plan when and where you are going to study, so you can create an effective study schedule that won't stress you out or leave you overly tired. If you are able to plan breaks between periods of study, you won't feel as drained at the end of the day, and you will be happier overall because you won't be working under such strenuous conditions.

Giving yourself time to relax also helps you avoid spending too much time on tedious tasks that are hurting, not enhancing, your productivity. When people are tired or stressed, they often spend hours doing mundane tasks so that they can feel they are being productive. I call this "productive procrastinating." You convince yourself you are being productive by doing stupid things like repeatedly checking your email, doing tasks that aren't really necessary, or trying to multitask.

> *Giving yourself time to relax also helps you avoid spending too much time on tedious tasks that are hurting, not enhancing, your productivity.*

62

This means that instead of being productive, you are draining your energy throughout the day on tasks that aren't helping you achieve your goals. If you give yourself time to relax, you will avoid spending hours on small and useless chores—you'll instead have the energy to spend more time on the meaningful tasks that improve your productivity. As Ernest Hemingway once eloquently said, "Never mistake motion for action."

Socializing

We humans have a natural tendency to want to be connected with others. That is why it is helpful to socialize in your free time. Socializing is a great way to have fun, make connections, and build your interpersonal skills. Hanging out with your friends at a restaurant or watching a movie is also a great way to de-stress.

But different people need different amounts of socialization. Interestingly, depending on whether you are an introvert or an extrovert, you will thrive in different working and social environments. Introverts thrive in quieter environments because they respond faster to dopamine and external stimulants, whereas extroverts require more stimuli in order to release and retain the same amount of dopamine.

This means that if an introvert and an extrovert were in the same situation (say going to an amusement park), the introvert would be the first to reach the quota of dopamine that is required for the feeling of "fun." A common misconception is that introverts are less social. This is not true. But introverts recharge themselves by spending time alone, whereas extroverts are recharged through the energy of others. For a more detailed explanation of introverts and extroverts, I would recommend reading *Quiet* by Susan Cain.

Knowing whether you are an introvert or an extrovert can be a significant help in figuring out how to surround yourself with the tools you need. A simplified way to determine whether you are more introverted or extroverted is to ask yourself, "At a party do I have a point where I need to go home, or do I like to stay till the end?"

This will help you reduce or increase your type and amount of socialization to fit your needs. If you are introverted, you many find hanging out with certain people is more tiring than hanging out with others. Different people have different energies, and you will react differently to each. You just have to experiment and see what is right for you.

And it is OK to want to go home and watch a little TV instead of going to Starbucks for the fifth time that week. Just make sure you are being balanced. Susan Cain created a really great system for balancing social life and downtime. She says to set a quota for the ideal number of times or hours you need to be with others per week. That way you will not feel pressured to go out more, but you will still have a balanced social life.

If you are an extrovert, you can use this in the opposite way. If you are one of those people who always wants to socialize and go out with friends, to the point where you never get anything done, you can set a limit on the number of hours you let yourself go out per week. This way you will know when you have surpassed your daily dose of socializing and it's time to start working.

Don't Drain Yourself—Instead Replenish

As mentioned before, it is important not to work so intensely for long periods that you burn out all your energy and then can't get anything done for the next week. That is not being productive, nor is it

"High-energy, fast-paced, extremely focused thinking is productive in the short-run, like for a test, but it isn't sustainable.

healthy. A way of keeping your energy level stable while working is to maintain the alpha state you learned before. Every time you take a break, pause before starting work again to do those quick exercises that will help you get back into the alpha state. Otherwise, you will be working in the beta state, which makes you tired really fast. Beta is the brain state you are in while completing a test or exam. Have you noticed how drained you feel afterward? High-energy, fast-paced, extremely focused thinking is productive in the short-run, like for a test, but it isn't sustainable. This is not how we should work in day-to-day life. If you consistently work in the beta state, you will be depleted so quickly you won't be able to get any substantial work done.

Sleep and Nature

Sleep. It sounds simple, doesn't it? Just sleep and you will de-stress. And it's true, if you sleep better, you will be less stressed. Sleep lowers blood pressure. Sleep replenishes your body. Sleep aids your memory (which is an important thing to keep in mind when you need to memorize information or a presentation). Sleep is just good. And I'll bet most of you enjoy it too. It's a win-win situation.

And the best thing about sleep is that it creates a cycle: Get more sleep. Reduce stress. Get better sleep because you are less stressed. But the opposite can also occur, which is what happens to most young adults today: Get less sleep because of work/commitments. Get more stressed. Get even less sleep because you are stressed (which causes insomnia).

> *Get more sleep. Reduce stress. Get better sleep because you are less stressed.*

If you have trouble sleeping, try to set regular sleep and wake-up times so you can get in the habit of going to bed at a reasonable hour and getting a full night's sleep. Eventually your brain and body will adjust to this schedule, and you will become accustomed to your sleep routine. (Don't forget to take into account the REM sleep cycles that you learned about earlier.)

Did you know that if you only had the choice between exercise and sleep, sleep would be better for your health? Sleep keeps us recharged for each new day that comes. While you sleep, your brain processes new information from the day. It goes through your memories from that day and puts them into your long-term memory. It is basically like backing up the files on your computer.

Getting the right amount of sleep for *you* is essential to becoming a master of productivity. Every individual is different, and the need for sleep varies from person to person. You have to find out how much sleep you require to thrive. The average is anywhere from seven to nine hours a night. I don't recommend getting less than that.

There are two groups of hormones and neurons that fight against each other to either keep you awake when you're awake or make you want to sleep during the night. Mid-afternoon is a time when the groups are at a stalemate, so you feel more tired. It is actually beneficial to give in to this feeling and take a short power nap when possible. You will be more productive and effective afterward.

So let yourself take a nap, and don't load up on caffeine to get you through the day—it will affect your sleep negatively. The recommended time for a nap is twenty-six minutes, and then you can get back to doing high-quality work. But if a nap is unrealistic, take two minutes and do some breathing exercises so your brain at least gets a break from work.

Follow this link to receive a free printout of the breathing exercises, as well as a step-by-step demonstration: www.productivity-master.com/resources. These exercises are also found on page 40 of this book.

A way to help ensure good-quality sleep is to turn off screens at least one hour before you go to bed. I know this may be hard, and I am guilty of using my phone or laptop right before I go to bed too. But the blue light emitted from devices like phones, laptops, or TV actually disturbs your sleep cycle and, therefore, lessens your quality of sleep. A way to reduce the blue light emission is to turn your phone to Night Mode at least an hour before you go to bed.

Charge your phone away from your bed so you're not tempted to check your phone right before bed or first thing in the morning. A bonus to this habit is that if you set your alarm on your phone and it's on the other side of the room, you will have to physically get up to turn your alarm off! So there's no hitting snooze. You are up and ready to start your day! Alternately, using blue-light filters can reduce the effects of light from screens if technology before you sleep is nonnegotiable.

The final technique to reduce stress is to surround yourself with nature or spend time in natural settings regularly. Nature and greenery, along with natural lighting, can have very beneficial effects on mental health. A study placed a mural of greenery inside a jail intake facility. It was found that this lowered fatigue and stress levels and increased mental resources, which illustrates the power of greenery, even in the form of art.

Humans are designed to admire and take comfort in natural forms and settings due to mirror neurons. Mirror neurons cause us to translate what we see into how we feel. This is what allows us to experience empathy. It is also how babies copy facial expressions. Next time you see a baby, make a face at them and watch—they will soon mirror your expression! (Your peers will subconsciously do the same.) It is important to be in close proximity to nature, greenery, and organic forms and materials (e.g., wood and stone), since they are known to help relieve stress.

Learning and Stress

If your job requires a lot of learning or you are in school, it is very important to be aware of your stress levels, because stressed brains don't work and learn as well as relaxed brains. An extreme example is someone freezing in panic during a presentation and not being able to speak. While your reaction to stress may not be this severe or visible, moderate stress still negatively impacts your productivity and learning ability.

Humans evolved by being on high alert, since we had to be prepared to react to threats very quickly or our lives would be in danger. When we encounter a situation that we interpret as dangerous or threatening, our brains release adrenaline and cortisol. This triggers the fight-or-flight reaction, which allows us to react to a life-threatening situation, but can be detrimental in the

"Our brains have been trained over generations to view change as a threat and to release cortisol and adrenaline to save us. So we now have to retrain our brains to realize that change (which is constant these days) is not a threat to our lives.

long term. Cortisol is the reason for chronic stress. While the fight-or-flight response is still important in certain situations, it is not necessary on a day-to-day basis, especially when it comes to tasks at work or school.

Our brains have been trained over generations to view change as a threat and to release cortisol and adrenaline to save us. So we now have to retrain our brains to realize that change (which is constant these days) is not a threat to our lives. Use the relaxation strategies and bring yourself into the alpha state every few hours or when you start a new task. This will help to reduce the amount of cortisol your brain releases and train your brain to calm down in stressful situations.

Body Controls Brain

I've already mentioned this, but I wanted to cover it again in this chapter because the information is so important and so easy to use to your advantage. Smile and sit up straight. That is it. You will start to automatically relax and feel happy because of the release of dopamine (responsible for happiness) and oxytocin (responsible for love).

Stop Multitasking

The last tip in this chapter is to stop multitasking! Multitasking does the opposite of what people think. It doesn't speed you up—it slows you down. Period. Multitasking may feel more productive because you're switching tasks at a fast pace, but it has been proven over and over again that focusing on one task at a time is much more productive than switching between several.

Switching between two tasks is like trying to be in two places at once. You will never enjoy yourself or be fully

> *Switching between two tasks is like trying to be in two places at once. You will never enjoy yourself or be fully present in either place, and it will take time to run between the two, hence distracting you from both places.*

present in either place, and it will take time to run between the two, hence distracting you from both places. The good news is that the solution is very simple. Once you have prioritized your tasks, do them in that order. And don't get distracted by your email or phone—instead, turn off notifications until you have completed the entirety of the task.

As for transitioning between tasks, Brendon Burchard, author of *High Performance Habits*, explains the process extremely well. He says that between tasks you should "release tension and set intention." This means that every time you transition from one task to another, you need to take a moment and release all the built-up tension from the last task—and then set your goals for the next. That way you will be able to start your new task with an open and fresh mind.

Take Action Summary

- Schedule time to relax.
- Find time for the amount of socializing that is right for you.
- Don't drain yourself—replenish yourself.
- Get good-quality sleep.
- Surround yourself with nature.
- Train your brain to reduce chronic stress.
- Remember that your body controls your brain: smile and sit up straight.
- Stop multitasking.

6 | Passion

Passion is the reason we do what we do—or at least it should be. So many people go through life without finding the reason they are here or what makes them happy. We go to work or school every day mindlessly doing tasks that we aren't happy doing. If we could all identify our passion early on, life would be so much fuller. Luckily, there are ways to help you figure out your passion, which I will explain throughout this chapter. Your passion is meant to fulfill your life as well as inspire others. Putting forth the effort to find your true passion will allow you to make a difference in your own life and the lives of others.

Hobbies and Skills

Building a career based on the hobbies and skills you love seems like a no-brainer. Yet people all over the world believe that their hobbies can't be turned into a job. And let me tell you, they are wrong. How do you think the circus was created? By defying the norm of what is considered a job, they built this amazing thing. Now I'm not suggesting you go out and start a circus to show off your hidden talents, but I am saying that anything is possible. You just have to look at it with a new perspective. And hey, if you are still stuck, you can always write a book on something—it worked for me!

As a Kid

In order to find a passion, look into what makes you happy. A lot of the time, your true passion is what you loved as a kid. This is not to say that *My Little Pony* is what you are meant to do with your whole life, but often things you loved as a kid can translate into real-life careers. Ask yourself, "What did I love when I was five? What was I interested in when I was five?" I realize you might find this a little silly, because it is quite likely that you don't remember what you were interested in when you were five, and even if you do, you probably had very unrealistic dreams. But even though they may seem unrealistic, they were big dreams, and you need to start creating big dreams again. Since nothing embarrassed you when you were young, anything is possible. A quote I love by Robin Sharma is "If people aren't laughing at your dreams, then you are not dreaming big enough!"

Looking back at what you loved as a kid is a great way to find out what you truly love to do. Try to remember what you were interested in before you were influenced by things like social expectations or parents' and peers' opinions. If you don't remember, ask your parents, aunts and uncles, or older siblings what they recall about your early interests.

Once you identify what you liked as a child, then you need to brainstorm and turn that into a career. For example, playing dress-up may translate into fashion. Legos into architecture. Toy cash register into accountant or actuary. Playing with trucks into car mechanic. Board game enthusiast into a job that involves strategy and problem solving. You can also remember subjects you excelled in during school and find careers related to that. It doesn't have to be a conventional career, by the way. You are allowed to research and generate your own ideas in order to create a life you will be happy with and that will bring you success.

Fire that Drives You

Everyone has something that drives them. Traveling. Writing. Singing. Dancing. Problem solving. Brain games. Math. Building. Designing. Business. Creating. Imagining. Everyone has that one thing that they would do without any other rewards (e.g., not just to get paid). Literally, anything can translate into a career. If you absolutely love traveling and writing, you can start a travel blog that combines your two passions. Or you can document your trip to a certain country and write a book about your travels. You will be able to live out your dreams, make money, and be productive and fulfilled all at once! There's always some passion that you can turn into a career as long as you put the effort into it.

Simon Sinek, who created the "Power of Why" movement, says that any successful business should first focus on why. What is their mission (not including money)? How do they want to change others' lives (and their own) for the better? This is what

73

you should think about every time you approach a task. How is this going to make others' lives and my own better? Why am I doing this? If you can't find any reason, you probably aren't focusing your energy in the right place, and you need to step back and figure out why you are doing what you do.

Another way to figure out your passion is to explore. Humans are designed to be curious, and we do well with trial and error. If you look at children, they are interested in everything, curious to see how the world works. When something doesn't work, they don't get too worried or try to obsessively make it work. Instead, they try something else. If you channel your childhood curiosity, you will open your mind to new perspectives and experiences that may lead you to your passion.

And it is important to note that your passion doesn't have to be something you're an expert in. Of course, it is helpful to have *some* knowledge, but you can quickly become proficient if you find a passion that drives you to explore and learn, because you will want to become an expert in it!

When you look at all the extremely successful people in the world, you will see one thing in common—no matter what field they specialize in, no matter their age or gender—the one thing that makes them all alike is their passion for what they are doing and their dedication to it.

Take Action Summary

- Find your passion.
    Think about how your hobbies and skills can translate into a career.
    Consider what you liked as a kid.
- Find the why—the passion that drives you.

7 | Take Action

A fter you put down this book for the last time, I have one final piece of advice: take action now. I have learned through experience that if we don't take action right away, we are never going to do it. So please, right now, take action and implement the strategies I've provided to you so you can start improving your life today. There is no better time to start than now. Once you convince yourself this is true, your life will change instantly.

If you train your brain to take action now, you will be conditioned to tackle things immediately in the future, without the thought of procrastination!

What you can do is go through the Take Action Summary pages for each chapter and make changes in your life immediately! You should practice the skills noted on the Take Action Summaries every day. You can even reread the book once, twice, or three times to truly absorb all the information and implement it in your life. The Take Action Summaries are located at the end of each chapter and are all summarized in the Appendix.

You can take notes on the things you learned and start incorporating these steps into your daily life. Don't worry if this feels overwhelming—I'm here to help. If you have any questions, please don't hesitate to contact www.productivity-master.com/contact. To optimize your productivity and access our resources, visit www.productivity-master.com and sign up for our free email list. You will get free tips and useful resources every week! You will also get updates on any programs we are offering and receive bonus material to help you become more productive, as well as the audio version of this book!

Thank You

Thank you so much for reading Path to Productivity and hearing my thoughts on productivity. I really hope these strategies have helped you become a more productive version of yourself. I would love to hear your feedback on the book or how the book has helped you become more productive in your life! You can email me at info@productivity-master.com. It would be greatly appreciated if you leave an amazing review on Amazon so you can help others become more productive too. And remember, as a gift, I am offering you the audio version of my book for free. Simply go to www.productivity-master.com and sign-up to my email list for immediate access. Thank you again, and have a very productive day!

Appendix

Alagapan, Sankaraleengam. *"Neurotransmitter - Dopamine."* LinkedIn SlideShare, 26 May 2011, www.slideshare.net/sankaraleengam/neurotransmitter-dopamine.

Bergland, Christopher. *"Exposure to Natural Light Improves Workplace Performance."* Psychology Today, Sussex Publishers, 5 June 2013, www.psychologytoday.com/us/blog/the-athletes-way/201306/exposure-natural-light-improves-workplace-performance.

Brann, Amy. *"3 More Ways to Use Neuroscience to Improve Your Productivity."* The Huffington Post, TheHuffingtonPost.com, 25 Nov. 2014, www.huffingtonpost.com/amy-brann/3-more-ways-to-use-neuros_b_5872574.html.

Brann, Amy. *"3 Ways Neuroscience Could Be Used in Your Organization to Improve Your Efficiency, Effectiveness and Productivity."* The Huffington Post, TheHuffingtonPost.com, 26 Oct. 2014, www.huffingtonpost.com/amy-brann/3-ways-neuroscience-could_b_5700880.html.

Breuning, Loretta Graziano. *Habits of a Happy Brain: Retrain Your Brain to Boost Your Serotonin, Dopamine, Oxytocin, & Endorphin Levels.* Adams Media, 2016.

Burchard, Brendon. *High Performance Habits.* Hay House, 2017.

Byrne, Rhonda. *The Secret.* Simon & Schuster, 2010.

Cain, Susan. *Quiet: the Power of Introvers in a World That Can't Stop Talking.* Broadway Books, an Imprint of the Crown Publishing Group, a Division of Random House, 2013.

Donovan, Laura. *"An Introvert's Brain vs. An Extrovert's Brain."* ATTN: ATTN: 23 Dec. 2015, www.attn.com/stories/4817/how-introverts-and-extroverts-are-different.

Eker, T. Harv. *"Why You Need To Focus On Your Strengths For A More Enjoyable & Successful Life."* T. Harv Eker Blog, Million Dollar Life Lessons, 24 Apr. 2018, blog.harveker.com/category/personal-development/productivity/.

Elrod, Hal. *The Miracle Morning - the 6 Habits That Will Transform Your Life before 8am.* Hodder & Stoughton General Div, 2017.

Errett, Jessica, et al. *"Effects of Noise on Productivity: Does Performance Decrease Over Time?"* University of Nebraska - Lincoln, Architectural Engineering -- Faculty Publications, digitalcommons.unl.edu/cgi/viewcontent.cgi?referer=&httpsredir=1&article=1012&context=archengfacpub.

Forleo, Marie. *"Brendon Burchard: How to Be Successful (Using Science)."* YouTube, YouTube, 19 Sept. 2017, www.youtube.com/watch?v=EG402k7vVZU.

Foxondavid. *"Neuro Expression."* Neuro Expression, 4 Aug. 2014, neuroexpression.wordpress.com/.

Guare, Richard, et al. *Smart but Scattered Teens: the Executive Skills Program for Helping Teens Reach Their Potential.* Guilford Press, 2013.

Kaufman, Scott Barry. *"STUDY ALERT: The Neuroscience of Grit and Growth Mindset."* Scott Barry Kaufman, 25 Apr. 2017, www.scottbarrykaufman.com/study-alert-the-neuroscience-of-grit-and-growth-mindset/.

Kenworthy, John. *"Your Brain on Stress and Anxiety."* YouTube, YouTube, 8 Nov. 2013, www.youtube.com/watch?v=gmwiJ6ghLIM&index=22&list=WL.

Kwik, Jim. *"Kwik Learning Online."* Kwik Learning, www.kwiklearningonline.com/.

Mode. *"This Is Your Brain on Space | Think | Little."* An International Architecture, Design, and Engineering Firm. Think, n.d. Web. 21 July 2017. <https://www.littleonline.com/think/this-is-your-brain-on-space>.

Postal, Karen. *"Exercise Helps You Think Better."* Karen Postal Ph.D., ABPP-CN, www.karenpostal.com/exercise-think-better/.

Sinek, Simon. *"How Great Leaders Inspire Action."* TED: Ideas Worth Spreading, Sept. 2009, www.ted.com/talks/simon_sinek_how_great_leaders_inspire_action.

Sussex, Tatyana. *"Does Listening to Music at Work Affect Your Productivity?"* LiquidPlanner, 22 June 2015, www.liquidplanner.com/blog/does-listening-to-music-at-work-affect-your-productivity/.

Widrich, Leo. *"The Science of How Temperature and Lighting Impact Our Productivity - The Buffer Blog."* Social, Buffer Social Blog, 22 Mar. 2016, blog.bufferapp.com/the-science-of-how-room-temperature-and-lighting-affects-our-productivity.

"Human Brain Anatomy 101 (with Pictures and Video)." Medical Information Illustrated, Medical Information Illustrated, 11 Sept. 2014, www.alilamedicalimages.org/2014/08/29/human-brain-anatomy/.

"Music's Effect on Learning [Infographic]." BroadyEdTech, 24 June 2013, digitallearningandteaching.wordpress.com/2013/06/24/musics-effect-on-learning-infographic/.

Must Reads

The Secret by Rhonda Byrne

High Performance Habits by Brendon Burchard

The 4-Hour Workweek by Timothy Ferris

The Miracle Morning by Hal Elrod

Quiet by Susan Cain

The Power of Why by Simon Sinek

Think and Grow Rich by Napoleon Hill

Habits of a Happy Brain by Loretta Graziano Breuning

Getting Thing Done by David Allen

Living The 80/20 Way by Richard Koch

Gratitude

I would like to thank my launch team. Without all of you, this book would not have been possible. You have been amazing and I have so much gratitude towards all of you. I would like to thank Joana Ceddia, Tess Chee, Lisa Chen, Rachel Cheung, Jason Gupta, Bobby Gupta, Sapna Humar, Jade Kagetsu, Chloe Lee, Ashley Leung, Golsa Makvandi, Alexandra Mallis, Angela Ng, Katelyn Ngo, Diya Ratti, Aarti Sabharwal, Tia Sato-Li, Julia Sen, Mitra Sen, Priyana Sen Smet, Liam Sharkey, Larry Smet, Julie Sue-A-Quan, Fiza Tagari, Ian Tan, Brynn Tauro, Briana Tse, Vanden Bos Family, Jennifer Zhang, and Angela Zhou for making up my launch team.

Notes

About the Author

Talina Sen Smet lives in Toronto, Canada and is the creator of www.productivity-master.com. She is a student and strong believer in productivity and how it can improve your life. Her goal is to help as many people as possible reach their potential through creating productive habits and reducing stress. Through research and daily practice, she has learned from the best thinkers on productivity and added her own distinctive ideas to this book and her website. Her belief that everybody has the potential to succeed drives her in her journey to teach people how to live their most productive life!

Get additional productivity tips and free resources at www.productivity-master.com.

Follow me on social media!
Facebook: @productivitymasters
Instagram: @productivity.master
Pinterest:@productivitymaster

Free Productivity Audiobook
A Gift to You!

As a gift, I would like to offer you the audio version of my book for free.

Simply go to **www.productivity-master.com** to claim your audiobook! Here, you can find more productvity resources for free!

Free Productivity Resources!

For more resources mentioned throughout the book such as "How to Plan Your Week in 5 Minutes - Whiteboard Layout", an editable schedule for your custom life, the LESS Goal Setting Chart, the Breathing Exercise Tutorial, and The Success Tracker Chart, visit www.productivity-master.com/resources.

How to Plan Your Week in 5 Minutes
Whiteboard Layout

www.productivity-master.com

Made in the USA
Columbia, SC
11 April 2019